DESKTOP

Bocce Ball

History, Rules, and Regulations

T0364027

RP Minis™
Hachette Book Group
1290 Avenue of the Americas, New York, NY 10104
www.runningpress.com
@Running_Press

First Edition: April 2020

Published by RP Minis, an imprint of Perseus Books, LLC, a subsidiary of Hachette Book Group, Inc. The RP Minis name and logo is a trademark of the Hachette Book Group.

The Hachette Speakers Bureau provides a wide range of authors for speaking events. To find out more, go to www.hachettespeakersbureau.com or call (866) 376-6591.

The publisher is not responsible for websites (or their content) that are not owned by the publisher.

ISBN: 978-0-7624-6944-4

Contents

INTRODUCTION

Instead of doing whatever it is you're doing, do this: clear off a little space on a nearby surface, grab your coworkers, family, or friends, and get the ball rolling with *Desktop Bocce Ball*! You've got the power of one of the world's favorite pastimes in your pocket: a global game that plays on a desk just the same!

Included in your *Desktop Bocce Ball* set are:

- eight teeny bocce balls (four per team!)
- an *even teenier* white *pallino* ball
- 10" x 14" felt playing mat to keep your game contained
- A cloth drawstring bag to house your bocce set
- Four small cones to demarcate a bocce league-style court/lane

THE PEOPLE'S GAME

Modern day bocce sightings include old folks slow-rolling a match in the park or a family getting a little too competitive in beach bocce, but this deceptively simple game actually has a long and storied history.

The first recorded instance of bocce is an ancient Egyptian painting of someone bending down to measure the distance of a close call. From there, we have evidence of bocce in ancient Greece. It was passed on to the Romans and was introduced throughout the empire. The game grew rapidly throughout Europe, and in the 1500s, the game became so popular that it started interfering with the productivity of soldiers and workers. Kings and queens across Europe took notice and began to ban the humble game. Surprising exactly no one, the ban did not work and Europeans continued to play, in one form or another, for the next 300 years.

During this period, Europeans introduced the sport across the world (along with various diseases) and many different versions and names arose for bocce, including:

- *bowls* (England)
- *volo* (Italy)
- *boules*, *pétanque*, *jeu provençal*, and *boule lyonnaise* (France)
- *bolas criollas* (Venezuela)
- *bocha* (Brazil)
- *bо́ćanje* (Serbia & Croatia)
- *balinanje* (Slovenia)

The first official bocce club was set up in the 1850s in France. The game, in all its variations, has since been played across the world by leisure-seekers, overly competitive amateurs, and professional players.

Ready to try your hand at the world's smallest iteration of this classic game? To get started, here's what you need to do:

- Unfold the felt playing mat and lay it on a flat surface

- Recruit players and pick teams: you'll want two teams of between one and four players each

- Assign a color (red or green) to each team and disperse the eight bocce balls accordingly

WHAT THE HECK IS A PALLINO?

Pallino means "cue ball" in Italian, though it doesn't function the same way your white cue ball does in a game of pool.

The pallino—which you might also hear called the target ball or jack—is the small white ball included in your bocce set. It is tossed or rolled onto the bocce court (in our case, the felt mat that comes in your box) and becomes the target for the game that follows. The player or team that gets their bocce ball closest to the pallino "holds point" and is the team to beat throughout a game of bocce.

How to Play and Score

There are a few variations on the game of bocce (more on that soon), but the objective of all variations is the same: place your team's balls, whether by bowling/rolling or throwing, closer to the pallino than your opponent does. The opposing team, during their subsequent turns, will then try to place their balls as close to the pallino as they can, too. One point is awarded to the team with the ball closest to the pallino, and one point is awarded for each of that team's balls that are closer to the pallino than the nearest of its opponent's balls.

- A team/player can knock the other team's balls out of the way to get a better shot at the pallino, or hit the pallino itself to move it into a better position.

- In the event of a distance dispute, use the mini ruler to accurately measure the distance between balls, the pallino, and other balls.

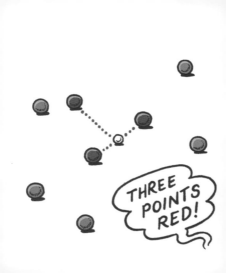

In particularly competitive games (especially when you're losing), you may feel tempted to try to hit your opponent's balls out of the way with each of your turns. In general, however, it is a poor strategy to try this on your team's last turn. It's often better to attempt to limit your damage by aiming your last shot as close to the pallino as possible and hoping that you thwart your opponent from scoring multiple points.

PRO TIP

A traditional bocce strategy is *boule devant*, *boule d'argent*, or "a ball in front is a money ball." Getting your ball to land in front of the pallino is extremely valuable, as it blocks the opposition from getting their balls close to the pallino. It may also cause the opposing team to accidentally hit your ball and push it closer to the pallino.

Rule
Variations

There are many styles of bocce, but here we'll cover two popular versions: traditional bocce, and a more familiar backyard-style bocce, both adapted for play using your itty-bitty desktop set.

No matter which version you choose to play . . .

- The pallino and both teams' balls must be played from the same edge of the mat. No part of the hand or fingers may cross the plane of the edge of the mat when throwing.

- If the pallino rolls off the felt lawn on its initial toss, re-do the shot to keep it on the playing mat. Decide before the game how you will handle the pallino ball if it rolls of the mat during play—maybe you let it go where it may, place it back on the mat near where it rolled off, or place it in a location equidistant for all balls currently on the mat. The choice is yours and depends on your location, just play fair, people!

- Decide before any game how you will handle bocce balls that roll or are bumped off the mat during play.

- To make your game more challenging, create a skinnier court on your playing mat using the cones included in your kit.

TRADITIONAL BOCCE

First team to 12 points wins

---

① Toss a coin or play rock-paper-scissors to decide which team plays out the pallino onto the play mat.

② The player that threw the pallino also throws the first ball. This team now "holds point," as they have the ball closest to the pallino.

③ The opposing team must then throw their balls until they "regain point" and get their ball closest to the pallino.

④ This process repeats until one team runs out of balls. At that point, the opposing team plays on and attempts to score further points.

⑤ When both teams have run out of balls, tally the points according to the scoring rules on pages 16–18 and collect all balls, including the pallino.

⑥ Each team should then alternate playing the pallino. Repeat steps 2–6 until one team reaches or exceeds 12 points.

BACKYARD BOCCE

**First team to 21 points wins, and the
winner must win by 2 or more points**

① To determine which team plays first,
one person from a team plays out the
pallino onto the play mat. That person
and another from the opposing team
play one ball each. Whichever team's
ball is closest to the pallino plays first.
All balls, including the pallino, should
be collected.

② The winning team of Step 1 plays the pallino onto the play mat.

③ The player that threw the pallino also throws the first ball.

④ Each team alternates throwing their balls until both teams run out of balls.

⑤ When both teams have run out of balls, tally the points according to the scoring rules on pages 16–18 and collect all balls, including the pallino.

⑥ If one team has not reached or exceeded 21 points, or they have but are not winning by 2 or more points, each team should then alternate throwing the pallino out. Repeat steps 3–6 until one team reaches or exceeds 21 points and wins by 2 or more points.

This book has been bound using handcraft methods and Smyth-sewn to ensure durability.

Box and interior illustrations by
Mario Zucca

Box and interior design by
Joshua McDonnell

Written by
Conor Riordan